Part One: Varied Assignments

Assignment 1   Which is the 'odd-man-out' in each of the following, and why?
(a) Violin, viola, cello, double bass, harp.
(b) Flute, oboe, clarinet, bassoon.
(c) Horn, trumpet, trombone, tuba.
(d) Xylophone, glockenspiel, snare drum, kettle drum, tubular bells.
(e) Piano, clavichord, harpsichord.

Assignment 2   Listen to the three extracts recorded on the cassette. As you listen to each piece of music, match one item from each column:

Tempo	Metre	Dynamic	Instrumentation	Century	Composer
slow	3 beats	loud	6 instruments plus percussion	17th	Tchaikovsky
moderate	4 beats	soft	string orchestra	18th	Stravinsky
fast	5 beats	varied	symphony orchestra	19th	Purcell
	changing			20th	Mozart

Assignment 3   For each of these countries name a famous composer, together with one of his or her important compositions:

Austria • France • Bohemia • Poland • Spain

Norway • USSR • Finland • USA • Hungary

Assignment 4   Which instruments do these jazz and pop musicians play?

John Dankworth	Pål Waaktaar	Eric Clapton
Benny Goodman	Chuck Berry	Stéphane Grappelli
Dave Brubeck	Dizzy Gillespie	Oscar Peterson
Jimi Hendrix	Lars Ulrich	Stewart Copeland
Louis Armstrong	Pete Townshend	Charlie Mingus
Ringo Starr	Tommy Dorsey	Rick Wakeman

Assignment 5   1   Vienna has the reputation of being one of the greatest musical cities in the world. Name two (or more) composers who lived and worked in Vienna:
(a) between 1750 and 1825
(b) between 1850 and 1890
(c) around 1910

2   Name a composition by each composer you have mentioned.

3

Assignment 6 Name, and explain, each of these musical signs, terms and abbreviations:

A

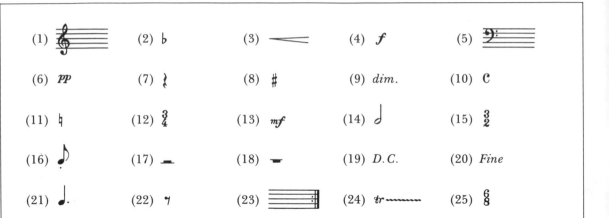

(1) 𝄞 (treble clef) (2) ♭ (3) ◁ (crescendo) (4) *f* (5) 𝄢

(6) *pp* (7) 𝄼 (8) ♯ (9) *dim.* (10) 𝄴

(11) ♮ (12) ¾ (13) *mf* (14) 𝅗𝅥 (15) 3/2

(16) ♪. (17) ▬ (18) ▬ (19) *D.C.* (20) *Fine*

(21) 𝅘𝅥. (22) 𝄾 (23) ‖: (repeat) (24) *tr* ⟿ (25) 6/8

B

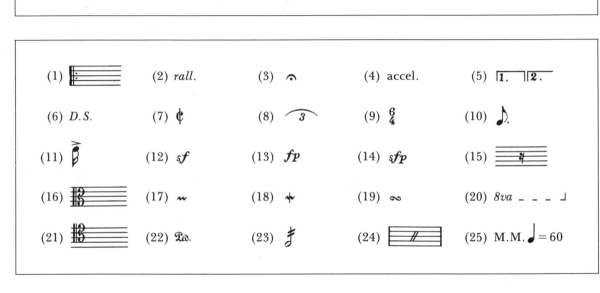

(1) :‖ (repeat) (2) *rall.* (3) ⌢ (pause) (4) accel. (5) |1. |2.

(6) *D.S.* (7) ¢ (8) ⌒3 (triplet) (9) 6/4 (10) ♪.

(11) 𝄿̂ (12) *sf* (13) *fp* (14) *sfp* (15) 𝄵

(16) 12/16 (17) ∿ (mordent) (18) ∿ (turn) (19) ∞ (20) *8va* _ _ _ ⌐

(21) 12/16 (22) 𝆮 (Ped.) (23) 𝄶 (24) 𝄍 (repeat) (25) M.M. 𝅘𝅥 = 60

Assignment 7 Give the title, and composer, of:

(a) a tone poem (or symphonic poem)
(b) a suite of incidental music
(c) a ballet suite
(d) a chorale prelude
(e) a programmatic piece for harpsichord or virginals
(f) a cantata
(g) a Passion
(h) a music-drama which includes leading-motives
(i) an operetta
(j) a Singspiel
(k) a concerto which has a title or a nickname
(l) a violin sonata which has a title or a nickname
(m) a string quartet which has a title or a nickname

Assignment 8   A   Identify each of these instruments:

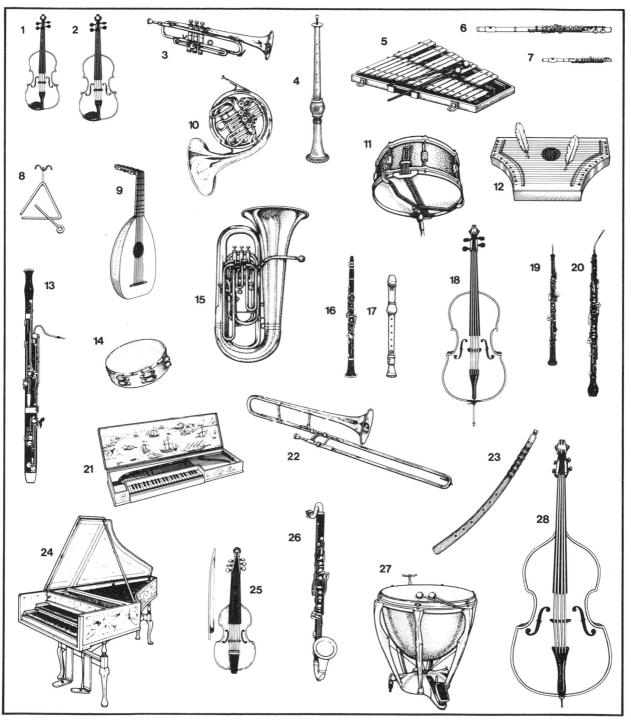

B   Which of these instruments would you be likely to hear:
   (a) on a record of 'Early Music';
   (b) in a performance of an orchestral suite or concerto by Bach;
   (c) in a symphony by Mozart;
   (d) in a symphonic poem by a late 19th-century composer.

Assignment 9 Contemporary music-making. Name:
(a) two professional orchestras based in London.
(b) two professional British orchestras based outside London.
(c) four non-British orchestras.
(d) two brass bands; and one military band.
(e) a famous choral society; a Cambridge college choir; and two other well-known choirs.
(f) four living orchestral conductors.
(g) two professional string quartets.
(h) a group specializing in the performance of 'Early Music'.
(i) two opera or ballet companies current in Britain; and three based outside Britain.
(j) three colleges of music in Britain; and two outside Britain.
(k) three important music festivals held in Britain each year; and two held abroad.
(l) an important pianoforte competition, held every three years in a northern English city.
(m) the present Master of the Queen's Musick.
(n) three other living British composers; and five of other nationalities.
(o) an important composition which has received its first performance during the past year or so.
(p) a musical which has been a 'hit' in the West End during the past year (name both composer and librettist if you can).
(q) a composer famous for writing film music; and another who specializes in music for TV (mention music by each composer).
(r) two pop groups or singers who have risen to the top of the charts during the last few weeks (give the title of each song).
(s) . . . still in connection with contemporary music-making – add, and give answers to, any important questions you think are missing from the above.

Assignment 10 **A** List these composers in chronological order:

| Mozart | Bach | Britten | Tchaikovsky | Beethoven | Stravinsky |

B After each name in your list, add the composer's nationality, his dates (from box 1), and the title of one of his compositions (from box 2).

1

| 1685–1750 | 1756–1791 | 1770–1827 |
| 1840–1893 | 1882–1971 | 1913–1976 |

2

| St Matthew Passion | The Rite of Spring | The Magic Flute |
| War Requiem | Fantasy-Overture: Romeo and Juliet | Fidelio |

C For each composer in your list, mention the title of another of his compositions which you have heard.

Assignment 11

soprano	•	mezzo-soprano	•	alto (contralto)
tenor	• countertenor	•	baritone	• bass

Match these famous singers to the voice-types given in the box above.

Peter Pears   Joan Sutherland   Dietrich Fischer-Dieskau
Kiri Te Kanawa   Marilyn Horne   Jessye Norman
Chaliapin   Placido Domingo   Marti Talvela
Janet Baker   Tito Gobbi   James Bowman
Gerard Souzay   José Carreras   Montserrat Caballé
Maria Callas   Teresa Berganza   Alfreda Hodgson
Enrico Caruso   Alfred Deller   Robert Tear
Kathleen Ferrier   Helen Watts   John Shirley-Quirk

Assignment 12

What is the difference between:
(a) a soprano and a mezzo-soprano;
(b) a countertenor and a tenor;
(c) a bass and a baritone.

Assignment 13

piano	violin	horn	cello	clarinet	organ
trumpet	saxophone	harpsichord	flute	guitar	sitar

For each instrument mentioned in the box, name two (or more) famous performers – past or present.

Assignment 14

For what kind of music-making is each of these famous?
The Royal Albert Hall   Glyndebourne   The Coliseum
The Wigmore Hall   Aldeburgh   Bayreuth
The Free Trade Hall (Manchester)

Assignment 15

overture	concerto	symphony	symphonic poem
piano sonata		trio sonata	piano quintet
song-cycle	madrigal	opera	oratorio cantata
étude for piano		variations for virginals	

Match the titles and nicknames below to the types of composition shown in the box above. Name the composer of each work.

(a) 'The Emperor'   (h) 'The Trout'
(b) *The King's Hunt*   (i) 'The Moonlight'
(c) *The Creation*   (j) *Danse Macabre*
(d) *The Silver Swan*   (k) *Dichterliebe*
(e) 'The Golden Sonata'   (l) *Carmina Burana*
(f) *The Hebrides (Fingal's Cave)*   (m) *Il Trovatore*
(g) 'The Drumroll'   (n) *La Campanella*

1   Which section of the orchestra plays the opening bars of the Theme?
2   In which bar are instruments from another section first heard?
     To which orchestral section do they belong?
3   In bars 11–13, do the double basses (a) descend by step, (b) rise by step,
     or (c) repeat the same note as a *pedal*?
4   Choose an Italian term to match the tempo of this music:
         Andante;   Allegro;   Vivace;   Presto.
5   The time signature has not been printed here. What should it be?
6   Name the tonic key of this music.
7   In which key is the music at bars 7 and 8?
8   Name a melodic device used in bars 7 and 8.
9   At which bar does the music return to the tonic key?
10   With which kind of cadence does Elgar end his Theme?
11   Elgar adds a great many details to his music, indicating to the
     performers exactly how the notes should be played. Explain each of
     these musical terms, signs and abbreviations which Elgar uses here:

12   In which musical form does Elgar design his Theme? Give the bar
     number where each section begins.
13   Name the interval formed by:
     (a) the first two notes of bar 1;
     (b) the last two notes of bar 7;
     (c) the upper two notes of bar 17;
     (d) the last two notes of bar 4;
     (e) the first two notes of bar 4.
14   Name two other compositions by Elgar.
15   Name two other composers who lived at the same time, and were of the
     same nationality as Elgar.

Assignment 17

1 Among the six tunes printed above identify:

a folksong	a duet by Mozart	a blues by W. C. Handy
a chorus by Handel	a Lied by Schubert	a chorale arranged by Bach

2 For each tune: (i) name the key, or mode, in which the tune is written;
(ii) supply the missing time signature;
(iii) state the number of beats to each bar.
3 Write out tune A one octave higher in the treble clef.
4 Write out tune B – and continue the tune for another four bars.

Assignment 18

In composing your own music, which signs, Italian terms or abbreviations would you include if you needed to indicate:

(a) slow
(b) fast, lively
(c) expressively
(d) smooth
(e) getting louder
(f) getting softer
(g) moderately
(h) slowing down gradually

Assignment 19

Plan a concert or recital of works of your own choice; either:
(a) an orchestral concert – including an overture, a concerto, a symphony, and one other work;
(b) a chamber concert – including a string quartet, a quintet, and one other work;
(c) a piano recital; or
(d) a Lieder recital.
Briefly introduce each composer, and write a programme note for at least one composition, introducing it to someone who has never heard it before.

9

Assignment 20

polonaise	allemande	minuet	courante	gavotte
csárdás	polka	tango	mazurka	gigue
pavan	sarabande	estampie	bourrée	waltz

(a) Of all the dances mentioned above, which is the oldest?

(b) Which would have been danced at the court of Henry VIII?

(c) Which was very popular at the court of Louis XIV, the 'Sun King' of France?

(d) Which dances formed the four main dance-movements of the Baroque keyboard suite?

(e) Which were sometimes also included in a suite as optional extra dances (or *galanterien*)?

(f) Which dance became the usual third movement of a Classical symphony?

(g) Which two dances would have been danced in the ballrooms of Vienna around 1875? Name a composer who wrote many examples.

(h) Which two dances are of Polish origin? Name a composer who wrote many examples for piano.

(i) Which dance is of Czech origin?

(j) Which is a national dance of Hungary? Name an example from a well-known ballet.

(k) Which dance came from Argentina?

Assignment 21

For each of these titles (1) mention what type of composition it is, and (2) give the name of its composer.

(a) Eine Kleine Nachtmusik

(b) Zadok the Priest

(c) Elijah

(d) Don Giovanni

(e) Don Juan

(f) The Four Seasons

(g) Now is the month of maying

(h) Tales from the Vienna Woods

(i) 'The Clock'

(j) The Washington Post

(k) The Erlking

(l) The Firebird

(m) Le Carnaval Romain

(n) Wachet auf

(o) The Planets

(p) The Entertainer

Assignment 22

In many pieces of *programme music*, it is necessary for the listener to know the 'programme' in detail, before listening, in order to appreciate fully how certain ideas are being portrayed in the music. There are some subjects, however, which are easier to depict than others. For example:

water •	birdsong •	a storm

A Mention one or more pieces of programme music depicting each of these ideas. How successful is each composer in achieving his aim?

B Select two of the pieces you have mentioned, and describe the musical means used by each composer to depict his chosen subject. For instance, think about: tempo, dynamics, instrumental colour, melody (or the lack of it), rhythm and flow, and so on.

Assignment 23

| string quartet | piano trio | clarinet quintet | violin sonata |

| string sextet | wind quintet | trio sonata |

How many players would take part in each of the above compositions?
Which instruments are likely to be involved in each one?

Assignment 24 Describe the differences between:

A (1) a viol and a violin
(2) a guitar and a sitar
(3) a brass band and a military band
(4) an operatic overture and a concert overture
(5) a minuet and a scherzo

B (1) a full anthem and a verse anthem
(2) strophic and through-composed (*durchkomponiert*)
(3) *recitativo secco* and *recitativo stromentato*
(4) polyphonic and homophonic textures

Assignment 25

Purcell	Schubert	Bach	Haydn
Bartók	Byrd	Schumann	Mozart	Chopin
Wagner	Britten	Machaut	Schoenberg
Handel	Grieg	Beethoven	Stravinsky	Tchaikovsky

A On a sheet of paper (turned sideways to give sufficient width) draw a chart beginning as the one shown below. Then add each composer mentioned in the box above to the appropriate column of your chart.

Medieval (to 1450)	**Renaissance** (1450–1600)	**Baroque** (1600–1750)	**Classical** (1750–1810)	**Romantic** (1810–1910)	**'Modern'** (20th Century)

B Also add to your chart five or six other composers whom you consider to be of similar importance.
C (This may involve some research.) Add the following writers, each to the appropriate column, at the bottom of your chart.

Shakespeare	Ibsen	Chaucer	Keats	Molière
Jane Austen	Thomas Hardy	Samuel Pepys	
Berthold Brecht	Charles Dickens	T. S. Eliot	

Assignment 26

(a) Prepare a column for your answers to this assignment by numbering from 1 to 24 down the left side of a sheet of paper.

(b) Listen to the extract of music recorded on the cassette, following the melody-line score.

(c) Listen again to the opening of the extract, and answer questions 1–3.

(d) Listen again to the complete extract, two or three times, and answer questions 4–17 printed on the score – selecting the correct answer from each set of boxes.

(e) Afterwards, answer questions 18–24, printed opposite.

1 Choose a suitable tempo marking to match the speed of this music:

   Very slow   Very moderately   Rather quickly

2 Select a suitable dynamic marking for bar 1: *p*   *mf*   *ff*   *sfz*

3 Choose a suitable expression marking, also for bar 1:
   passionately; *sweet and expressive*; *rather heavily*; *crisp and clear.*

4 The instrument playing the melody is

   a piccolo   a flute   an oboe   a clarinet

5 The melody instrument is   accompanied   unaccompanied

6 The harp plays

   chords   an arpeggio   a glissando

8 These notes are played by a

   horn   trumpet   trombone   tuba

7 The strings first enter in

   bar 4   bar 5   bar 6

9 The accompanying strings are played

   pizzicato   col legno   tremolo

10 The instrument taking over the melody is

   an oboe   a trumpet   a saxophone

12

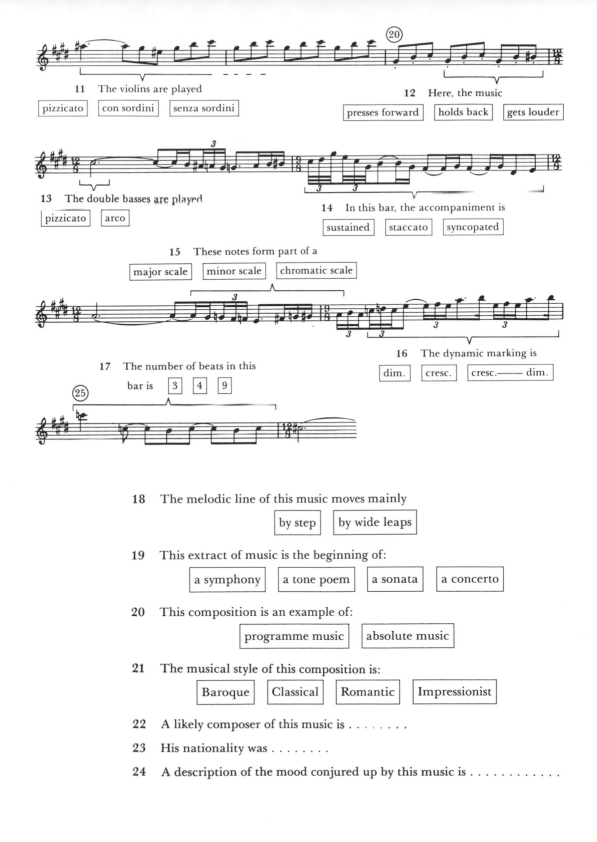

11   The violins are played

| pizzicato | con sordini | senza sordini |

12   Here, the music

| presses forward | holds back | gets louder |

13   The double basses are played

| pizzicato | arco |

14   In this bar, the accompaniment is

| sustained | staccato | syncopated |

15   These notes form part of a

| major scale | minor scale | chromatic scale |

16   The dynamic marking is

| dim. | cresc. | cresc.——— dim. |

17   The number of beats in this bar is

| 3 | 4 | 9 |

18   The melodic line of this music moves mainly

| by step | by wide leaps |

19   This extract of music is the beginning of:

| a symphony | a tone poem | a sonata | a concerto |

20   This composition is an example of:

| programme music | absolute music |

21   The musical style of this composition is:

| Baroque | Classical | Romantic | Impressionist |

22   A likely composer of this music is . . . .

23   His nationality was . . . .

24   A description of the mood conjured up by this music is . . . .

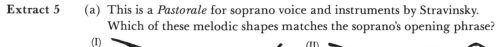 **Assignment 27**   Listen to the five varied extracts of music recorded on the cassette.
For each extract, there are three questions.

Extract 1   (a) Which of the following matches the style of this music?
  alla marcia;   *alla turca*;   *tempo di valse*.
  (b) Is this music played by a brass band, military band, or full orchestra?
  (c) How many beats to a bar are there in this music?

Extract 2   (a) Two instruments of the same kind play the first tune. Which instruments
  are they?
  (b) Which of these Italian terms matches the speed of this music?
  Largo;   *Andante*;   *Vivace*;   *Prestissimo*.
  (c) The composer is French – but he is writing a 'Spanish dance'. How does
  he bring a Spanish flavour to this music?

Extract 3   (a) Choose a time signature to match this music:

$$\frac{2}{4} \qquad \frac{3}{4} \qquad \frac{4}{4} \qquad \mathbf{\large ¢}$$

  (b) Which of these titles best suits this piece?

  | Scherzo | Nocturne | Fugue | Waltz |

  (c) Which of the following instrumental groups plays this music?

  | brass group | woodwind group | brass and woodwind mixed |

Extract 4   (a) On which of these keyboard instruments is this music played?

  | chamber organ | virginals | clavichord |

  (b) This piece is in three short sections, each played twice. Which of these
  musical devices is heard at the beginning of each section?
  sequence;   *imitation*;   *inversion*.
  (c) In which of these centuries was this music composed?
  16th   18th   20th

Extract 5   (a) This is a *Pastorale* for soprano voice and instruments by Stravinsky.
  Which of these melodic shapes matches the soprano's opening phrase?

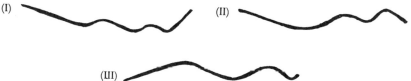

  (b) Which of the following describes the bass-part (played by a bassoon)?
  walking;   drone;   off-beat   ostinato.
  (c) Name two other instruments accompanying the voice.

📼 **Assignment 28**   Listen to the five varied extracts of music recorded on the cassette.
For each extract, there are three questions.

Extract 1   (a) The first tune is played by violins, then repeated. Is it now played:
an octave higher;   an octave lower;   or at the same pitch?
(b) Name two woodwind instruments heard during the second tune.
(c) This is a march-tune by one composer, arranged and orchestrated by
another. Is the music:
(i) by Mozart, arranged by Britten;
(ii) by Rossini, arranged by Mozart;
or (iii) by Rossini, arranged by Britten?

Extract 2   (a) Choose an Italian term to match the speed of this music:
Andante;   *Adagio*;   *Allegro*.
(b) In this music, which of the following Italian terms would be printed:
(i) below the violin parts;
and (ii) below the parts for lower strings?

| pizzicato | glissando | con sordino | col legno |

(c) During which of these periods would this music have been composed?
Renaissance;   Baroque;   Classical;   Romantic.

Extract 3   (a) Music for singer and a small group of instruments. Which of the
following describes the effect made by the bowed string instrument?

| riff | drone | syncopation | imitation |

(b) What other types of instruments are taking part?
(c) From which of these countries does this music come?
Africa;   China;   India;   West Indies.

Extract 4   As you listen to this extract, choose one item to match the music from each
column:

(a)	Tempo (speed)	(b)	Style and expression	(c)	Instrumentation
	moderate		agitated, vigorous		harp, oboe, violin
	very slow		playful		guitar, flute, cello
	quite brisk		smooth and flowing		harp, flute, viola

Extract 5   (a) Which of the following matches the style of the opening of this piece?

| ragtime   blues   trad. jazz   rhythm 'n' blues |
| boogie-woogie   country and western   reggae |

(b) Of which well-known tune is this an arrangement?
(c) After the opening chorus, a five-note phrase is often repeated. Which of
these terms describes this repeated phrase?
fugato;   break;   riff;   ground;   coda.

Overture: *Le Carnaval Romain*   *Berlioz (1803–1869)*
(Roman Carnival)

mf espressivo

1 Which of the following instruments plays the melody in this extract?

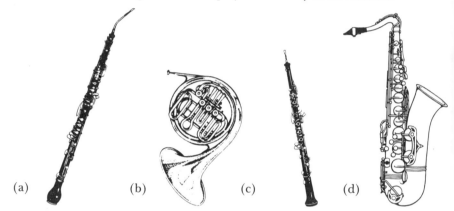

(a)   (b)   (c)   (d)

2 Name the instrument.
3 Which section of the orchestra provides the accompaniment?
4 Describe the way in which these instruments are played at the beginning
   of the extract.
5 In which bar are flutes first heard?
6 The time signature is missing from this music. What should it be?
7 Is this music in the major key, or the minor key?
8 Name the key.
9 Which of the following matches this music?

| *Adagio pesante* | *Andante sostenuto* | *Allegro scherzando* |

🔘 **Assignment 30**

Recorded on the cassette are three pairs of extracts. Listen to one of these
pairs, two or three times. Compare the two extracts of music, and comment
on their similarities and differences.

For example, these could include:

| instrumentation   tempo (speed)   rhythm   melody   mood |
| any special instrumental effects   concordant/discordant |
| dynamic level   major, minor; tonal, atonal |
| period or century of composition   any other points of interest |

Mahler was inspired to write this music by a satirical drawing of an animals' funeral procession. Stags carry the coffin, upon which sits a fox. Hares gleefully wave flags. There is a band of musicians – cats, frogs, crows. And other birds fly above. The corpse, inside the coffin, is that of a hunter. . .

1   Which kind of drum is heard solo in bars 1 and 2?

2   Which of the following instruments enters solo in bar 3?

trumpet	•	trombone	•	violin	•	double bass

3   In which bar does another instrument enter with the same tune? Name the instrument.

4   Which of these instruments enters with the tune in bar 15?

bass tuba	•	harp	•	clarinet

5   Name the instrument which enters with fanfare-like phrases in bar 19. Are its opening notes played *legato*, or *staccato*?

6   Which of these instruments enters with the tune at bar 23?

flutes	•	oboes	•	clarinets	•	saxophones

7   Is this music in the major key, or the minor key?

8   Name the key.

9   Mahler bases this funeral march upon a transformation of a well-known tune. Name that tune.

10 How is the original tune transformed or altered?

11 Listen to this extract again, and describe how Mahler makes use of each of these musical devices:
    (i) canon
    (ii) ostinato

Assignment 32

(1) Monteverdi	(4) Weber	(7) Smetana	(9) Puccini
(2) Purcell	(5) Wagner	(8) Bizet	(10) Britten
(3) Mozart	(6) Verdi		

(a) List, in a single column, the opera composers given in the box above.

(b) To each name in your list add the composer's nationality, and the title of one his operas, chosen from the box below.

Carmen	*Peter Grimes*	*Dido and Aeneas*	*Orfeo*
La Bohème	*The Marriage of Figaro*		*The Bartered Bride*
Die Meistersinger		*Il Trovatore*	*Der Freischütz*

(c) To your list add two other composers of opera, giving the nationality of each, and the title of one of his or her operas.

Assignment 33

Name a composer well known for writing:

(a) fugues
(b) string quartets
(c) Lieder
(d) piano sonatas
(e) piano concertos
(f) cantatas
(g) oratorios
(h) études for piano
(i) ballets
(j) operettas
(k) concert overtures
(l) pieces structured on a ground bass
(m) compositions using serial techniques
(n) musicals (or musical comedies)

Assignment 34

Give the English meaning of each of these Italian terms connected with tempo (speed, or pace):

adagio	allegro	allegretto	largo
vivace	andante	andantino	prestissimo
rall. rit.	meno mosso	più mosso	a tempo

Assignment 35

Give the English meaning of each of these Italian terms describing mood, style, or expression:

cantabile	appassionato	grazioso	sostenuto
agitato	maestoso		staccato
dolce con fuoco	tranquillo	leggiero	scherzando

Assignment 36

| Pathétique | Emperor | Pastoral | London | Jupiter |

Each of these titles or nicknames is shared by at least two compositions by different composers. In each instance, mention both compositions (adding as much information as you think necessary) together with the name of each composer.

18

The splendour falls on castle walls
And snowy summits old in story:
The long night shakes across the lakes,
And the wild cataract leaps in glory:
Blow, bugle, blow, set the wild echoes flying,
Bugle, blow; answer, echoes, answer, dying.

O hark, O hear, how thin and clear,
And thinner, clearer, farther going!
O sweet and far from cliff and scar
The horns of elfland faintly blowing!
Blow, let us hear the purple glens replying:
Bugle, blow; answer, echoes, answer, dying.

O love they die in yon rich sky,
They faint on hill or field or river:
Our echoes roll from soul to soul
And grow for ever and for ever.
Blow, bugle, blow, set the wild echoes flying;
And answer, echoes, answer, dying.

This music is composed for a solo voice, a solo instrument, and a string orchestra. Listen to the piece, following the words.

Then listen two or three times more, discovering answers to these questions:

1   At the beginning, which Italian word would be printed beneath the parts for the cellos and double basses?
2   Which type of voice sings the words?

contralto	countertenor	tenor	baritone	bass

3   During the two lines beginning 'Blow, bugle, blow,' solo voice and solo instrument echo and answer each other. Name the instrument.
4   Describe the string accompaniment during these two lines.
5   Which instruments of the string orchestra do not play at the beginning of verse 2?
6   During the last two lines of verse 2, how is the sound of the solo instrument changed from before?
7   How does the music of verse 3 provide a contrast to that of verse 2?
8   Describe how Britten builds up tension during the music during the last two lines of the poem. How is the tension released?
9   During this piece there are several examples of *word-painting*. Describe how Britten 'paints' these ideas in his music:
    (a) 'Blow, bugle, blow,'
    (b) 'dying. . .'
10 Pick out another example of word-painting, and describe how Britten brings out the meaning of the words.
11 Is this music: serial (12-note); mainly in a major key; or modal throughout?

The recording on the cassette of this blues, performed by Jelly Roll Morton and His Red Hot Peppers, was made in Chicago, 21 September 1926. The music is played by a seven-piece ensemble: cornet, clarinet, trombone (Edward 'Kid' Ory), piano ('Jelly Roll' Morton), banjo, string bass and drums, joined at one point by two extra clarinets.

The recording begins, unusually, with some comic spoken dialogue. Then, after a droll eight-bar introduction, there follow seven choruses, each one based on this 12-bar blues pattern:

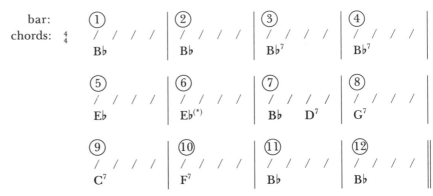

[* In some choruses, E♭ minor]

Dead Man Blues has three themes or 'strains': A, B and C. This plan shows how the piece is structured:

Section	12-bar chorus	Content
Introduction		8 bars
A^1	1	ensemble, in collective improvisation
A^2	2	solo 1
B^1	3	solo 2
B^2	4	solo 2 continued
C^1	5	three clarinets in harmony
C^2	6	three clarinets, plus countermelody
A^3	7	ensemble, in collective improvisation
Coda		2 bars

1   Listen to *Dead Man Blues*, following the plan of the music outlined above.

2   Listen to this blues again, discovering answers to these questions:
   (a) Which famous tune is hinted at during the introduction?
   (b) Which instrument plays solo 1? Which instruments accompany?
   (c) Which instrument plays solo 2?
   (d) Which instrument plays the countermelody in chorus 6?
   (e) On which theme – A, B or C – is the coda based?

3   Listen again to choruses 5 and 6, following the 12-bar blues pattern above. In which bars do the percussive 'crashes' occur? On which beat?

Third movement from *Music for Strings,*   Bartók *(1881–1945)*
Percussion and Celesta*

This is an example of what Bartók called 'night-music', suggesting an impression of nature-sounds – insects, night-birds, whispering leaves and grasses – heard in the stillness of the night. Below, is a diagrammatic score of the first part of this movement, indicating some of the main musical events. This part of the movement is built up in nine sections (approximate timing of each section is given here in seconds).

1   Investigate the score; then listen to the music, following the score.

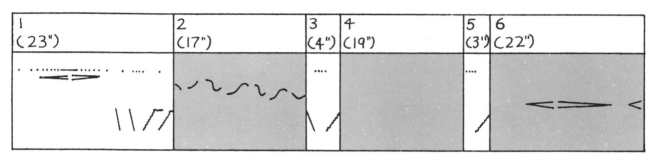

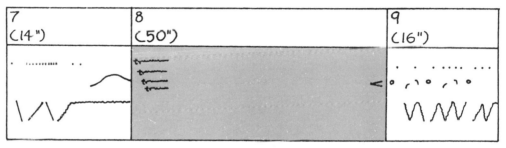

2   Listen to the music again, and answer these questions:
(a) Name the percussion instrument heard at the beginning of Section 1.
(b) Name the next instrument – and also the special effect being produced.
(c) During Section 2, which of the following play short melodic phrases?

| violins | violas | double basses |

(d) On which instrument is a roll played throughout Section 4?
(e) With which of these musical devices does Section 6 begin?
        imitation;   *sequence*;   *inversion*.
(f) Name two instruments heard for the first time during Section 8.
(g) Describe the mood presented by the music of Section 8.
(h) Which four of these percussion instruments are heard during Section 9?

| kettle drum | woodblocks | tubular bells | piano | tam tam |
| glockenspiel | xylophone | celesta | vibraphone |

3   Listen again to Section 8. Draw your own detailed diagrammatic score – but use a rectangle much bigger than that shown in the score above.

Assignment 40

Palestrina | Dowland | Vivaldi | D. Scarlatti

Chopin | Verdi | Wolf | Mahler | R. Strauss

Match each composer to the particular type of composition for which he is most famous:

operas	motets and masses	Lieder	lute ayres
symphonies	concertos	tone poems
music for piano	music for harpsichord

Assignment 41   *Intermezzo* from 'Hassan'   *Delius (1862–1934)*

Andante e molto tranquillo

1 Which instrument is heard playing solo at letter **A**?

2 The phrases at **B**, **C** and **D** are played by flute, oboe and clarinet – but in which order are these three instruments heard?

3 Which instrument plays the phrase beginning at letter **E**? Has this instrument a single reed, a double reed, or no reed at all?

4 Name the instrument which plays the melody at letter **F**. Which instrument is prominent in the accompaniment in this bar?

5 Which ornament is missing in the score at bar 11? How many notes are played by the double basses in the same bar? Are these notes played *pizzicato*, or *arco*?

6 Name the instruments which play the two phrases at **G** and **H**. What do these two instruments have in common?

7 In which bar after letter **H** is the harp next heard playing a falling and rising arpeggio?

8 Name the instrument which plays the melody at letter **I**. In the same bar, which instrument quietly plays two notes *con sordino*?

9 Towards the end of the piece, a roll is played quietly on a kettle drum. At which bar does this roll begin?

1   Name the instruments which in turn are featured solo, playing this idea:

2   Which particular type of Baroque concerto is this – a solo concerto, or a concerto grosso?

3   In a Baroque concerto of this type, what name is given to the group of soloists?

4   What name is given to the string orchestra?

5   Name the keyboard instrument involved in this piece. What name is given to the part it plays in this music?

6   In which of the following musical forms is this movement likely to be structured?

> *ternary form*   *sonata form*   *ritornello form*   *variations*

7   Which of the following terms best describes the music for bars 1–8?

first subject • ground • ritornello • episode

8   Are these bars (1–8) played by the string orchestra alone, or do the solo instruments also join in?

9   During this extract, the appearances of *X* are separated by other musical material. Is this material, on each occasion, quite new – or is it always taken from the opening bars?

10   Does *X* always appear in the tonic key? On which occasion is *X* presented in a varied version?

Assignment 43   Listen to the six varied extracts of music recorded on the cassette, gathering information and discovering answers to the questions on each extract.

Extract 1   (a) Is this music in the major key, or the minor key?

(b) How many beats are there to each bar?

(c) From each of these sections of the orchestra, name one instrument taking part in this music:

| woodwind | brass | percussion |

(d) Which instrument plays the *continuo* part?

(e) During which of these periods in the history of music was this piece composed?

| Baroque | Classical | Romantic | 20th century |

(f) Suggest a likely composer.

(g) What kind of mood does this music present?

(h) Is this a movement from a sonata, a suite, or a concerto?

Extract 2   (a) Name the solo instrument playing in this extract.

(b) To which section of the orchestra does it belong?

(c) Select the time signature which best suits this music:

$$\frac{2}{4} \qquad \frac{6}{8} \qquad \frac{4}{4} \qquad \frac{5}{4}$$

(d) What name is given to the type of composition from which this extract is taken?

(e) In which of these centuries was this music composed?

| 16th century | 18th century | 20th century |

(f) Suggest a likely composer.

(g) Towards the end of the extract, which of these musical devices is heard in the string parts?

| ostinato | sequence | imitation | inversion |

Extract 3   (a) Which of the four sections of the orchestra does not take part in this extract?

(b) Which of these terms matches this music?

| major | minor | modal | atonal |

(c) During which century is this music likely to have been composed?

(d) Which of the following correctly describes the group of percussion instruments taking part?

    (i) all tuned percussion;

    (ii) all non-tuned percussion;

    (iii) a mixture of tuned and non-tuned.

(e) Name four of the percussion instruments taking part.

(f) What do you like or dislike about this music?

24

Extract 4   (a) Which of these types of voice do you hear during this extract?

| soprano | contralto | tenor | baritone | bass |

(b) Name an instrument, not played with a bow, which is prominent in the accompaniment.

(c) Is this music from an oratorio, an opera, a mass, or a cantata?

(d) During which of these periods was this music composed?

| Baroque | Classical | Romantic |

(e) Which of the following is most likely to be the composer?
  Monteverdi;   Bach;   Mozart;   Puccini;   Britten.

Extract 5   (a) Which of these rhythms is repeated at the beginning of this extract?

(i) ‖: 𝅗𝅥 𝅘𝅥𝅮𝅘𝅥𝅮 :‖   (ii) ‖: 𝅗𝅥 𝅘𝅥 𝅘𝅥 :‖   (iii) ‖: 𝅘𝅥 𝅘𝅥 𝅘𝅥 :‖

(b) What name is given to this musical device – in which a rhythmic or melodic pattern is obstinately repeated, over and over?

(c) Which of these time signatures best suits the rhythm?

$\frac{3}{4}$ $\frac{4}{4}$ $\frac{2}{2}$ $\frac{6}{8}$

(d) Does the time or metre stay the same throughout the extract, or does it change?

(e) During which of these periods was this music composed?

| Renaissance | Classical | Romantic |

(f) Is this music most likely to have been played in an ordinary home, a church, or a castle?

Extract 6   (a) The introduction to this piece is a tongue-in-cheek impression of a train. Which kind of instrument makes low-pitched rasping sounds as the train starts and begins to pick up speed?

(b) Which of these instruments eventually plays the melody?

| 3 clarinets | 4 trumpets | 5 saxophones |

(c) The melody is repeated. Which solo instrument now adds 'comments'? What accounts for the special sound it is making?

(d) A short 'B section' follows; then the main melody returns. It has three phrases. Are they all different – or are any the same?

(e) Which instrument (on the right) next plays a jazzy solo? Is it a horn, trombone, double bass, or bass guitar?

(f) Which of the following describes the bass part?

| walking | drone | off-beat |

(g) Another solo is heard (on the left). Is it played by a clarinet, trumpet, or saxophone?

(h) Which of these time signatures matches this music?

$\frac{3}{4}$ $\frac{4}{4}$ $\frac{6}{8}$

(i) Which of the following best suits the style of this music?

| blues | ragtime | swing | rock'n'roll |

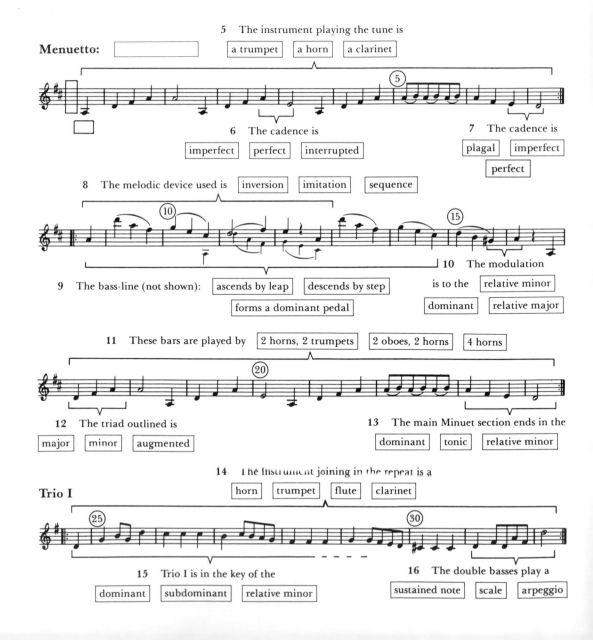

Assignment 44   (a) Prepare a column for your answers to this assignment by numbering from 1 to 31 down the left side of a sheet of paper.

(b) Listen to the recording of the music on the cassette, following the melody-score. Then answer questions 1–4.

(c) Listen to the music again (twice through – with the tape paused at the end of each section) and answer questions 5–24 printed on the score – selecting the correct answer from each set of boxes.

(d) Afterwards, answer questions 25–31, printed opposite.

1   Choose a suitable tempo marking for this music:
Largo;   *Adagio*;   *Allegretto*;   *Presto*;   *Prestissimo*.

2   The time signature has not been printed on the score. What should it be?

3   Select a suitable dynamic marking for bar 1:   *pp*   *mf*   *ff*   *fp*

4   Name the tonic key of this music.

5   The instrument playing the tune is

Menuetto:

a trumpet   a horn   a clarinet

6   The cadence is

imperfect   perfect   interrupted

7   The cadence is

plagal   imperfect

perfect

8   The melodic device used is   inversion   imitation   sequence

9   The bass-line (not shown):   ascends by leap   descends by step

forms a dominant pedal

10   The modulation is to the   relative minor

dominant   relative major

11   These bars are played by   2 horns, 2 trumpets   2 oboes, 2 horns   4 horns

12   The triad outlined is

major   minor   augmented

13   The main Minuet section ends in the

dominant   tonic   relative minor

14   The instrument joining in the repeat is a

horn   trumpet   flute   clarinet

Trio I

15   Trio I is in the key of the

dominant   subdominant   relative minor

16   The double basses play a

sustained note   scale   arpeggio

17 The melodic device used is

| sequence | inversion | repetition |

18 The ornament is an

| acciaccatura | appoggiatura |

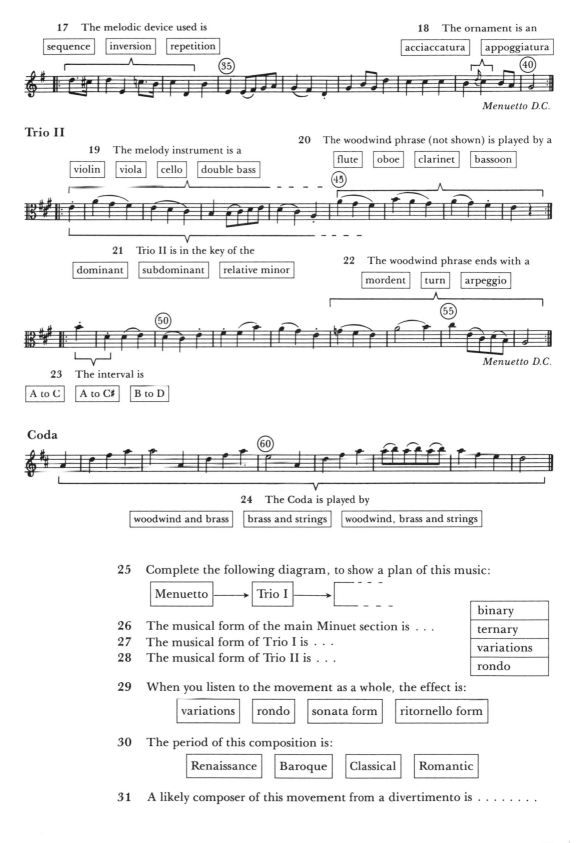

Menuetto D.C.

Trio II

19 The melody instrument is a

| violin | viola | cello | double bass |

20 The woodwind phrase (not shown) is played by a

| flute | oboe | clarinet | bassoon |

21 Trio II is in the key of the

| dominant | subdominant | relative minor |

22 The woodwind phrase ends with a

| mordent | turn | arpeggio |

23 The interval is

| A to C | A to C♯ | B to D |

Menuetto D.C.

Coda

24 The Coda is played by

| woodwind and brass | brass and strings | woodwind, brass and strings |

25 Complete the following diagram, to show a plan of this music:

Menuetto ⟶ Trio I ⟶ ⬚

| binary |
| ternary |
| variations |
| rondo |

26 The musical form of the main Minuet section is . . .

27 The musical form of Trio I is . . .

28 The musical form of Trio II is . . .

29 When you listen to the movement as a whole, the effect is:

| variations | rondo | sonata form | ritornello form |

30 The period of this composition is:

| Renaissance | Baroque | Classical | Romantic |

31 A likely composer of this movement from a divertimento is . . . .

27

Assignment 45

1 In choral music, what do the abbreviations S.A.T.B. refer to?
2 How many movements usually make up (a) a symphony by Haydn, and (b) a concerto by Mozart?
3 Which of the following instruments have reeds?

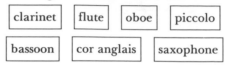

| clarinet | flute | oboe | piccolo |

| bassoon | cor anglais | saxophone |

4 What is the name given to music composed to introduce the acts or scenes of a play, perhaps to accompany certain scenes, or to be played while the curtain is down and the scenery is being changed?
5 Name a programme symphony by Berlioz.
6 Give the title of a composition in nationalist style. Name its composer, and mention his country of birth.
7 Name a keyboard instrument, other than the harpsichord, in which the strings are plucked.
8 Name a keyboard instrument, other than the piano, in which the strings are struck.
9 Name two composers of piano music who were also virtuoso pianists.
10 Explain the difference between these two time signatures:

$$\mathbf{C} \quad \mathbf{\mathbb{C}}$$

Assignment 46

1 Name two composers, other than J. S. Bach, who were born in the year 1685.
2 Which of the following percussion instruments are 'pitched' or 'tuned'?

| kettle drum • snare drum • bass drum • triangle |
| glockenspiel • cymbals • tambourine • xylophone • celesta |

3 Which of the percussion instruments in the box above would you expect to hear in a symphony by Mozart?
4 In the history of the symphony, who replaced the *minuet* with the *scherzo*?
5 With which particular instrument do you associate:
   (a) Liszt   (b) Paganini   (c) Couperin   (d) Dowland   (e) Leutgeb
6 Name a composition by Rimsky-Korsakov which demonstrates his gift for orchestration and his brilliant use of orchestral timbres.
7 Suggest time signatures which a composer might use to indicate:
   (a) simple triple time;
   (b) simple quadruple time;
   (c) compound duple time.
8 In which type of music are the following likely to be involved?
   sine wave generators;   *ring modulators*.
9 Give the names of two 20th-century Russian composers of symphonies.
10 Complete the following pairs:
   _____ and Sullivan   Rodgers and _____   _____ and Loewe
   Lennon and _____   Tim Rice and _____

Assignment 47

1. Which three orchestral woodwind instruments have a double reed?
2. Describe the effect a mute is likely to have on the sound of:
   (a) a violin;
   (b) a trumpet.
3. Give the title of a famous collection of Tudor music for virginals.
4. Give the title of a famous collection of madrigals.
5. Identify each of these different types of scale:

6. Why does a bassoon sound lower notes than an oboe?
7. Why do the strings of a violin produce higher sounds than those of a cello?
8. Name two sons of J. S. Bach.
9. Name a Spanish composer, together with the title of one of his or her compositions.
10. In jazz what is (i) a riff, and (ii) a break?

Assignment 48

1. Name two instruments likely to play a *continuo* part in a work by Bach.
2. Name the next note in this harmonic series:

3. Name the first important composer of opera, and give the title of one of his operas.
4. Name the notes which form each of these triads or chords in G major:
   (i) tonic;
   (ii) dominant;
   (iii) subdominant;
   (iv) supertonic.
5. What is meant by 'secular music'?
6. Name a composer famous for writing music in polychoral style.
7. Name a composer of pieces for 'prepared piano'.
8. Explain the meaning of 'tonic pedal'.
9. Name a *Lied* by Schubert which is in strophic form, and another which is *durchkomponiert* (or through-composed).
10. What is the essential difference between music which is *polytonal* and music which is *atonal*?

Assignment 49 (a) What is the full name of the 'piano'?
(b) Explain the reason for this name.
(c) Who invented the piano?
(d) Name two other piano-makers who later made important contributions to the development of the instrument.

Assignment 50 1 Listen to the seven extracts of piano music recorded on the cassette. Match each extract to a composer in the box:

Haydn	•	Chopin	•		Beethoven
Prokofiev	•	Liszt	•	Cage	• Debussy

2 Which two extracts did you find most interesting?
Describe the difference in piano style between your two chosen extracts – for instance, think about:

the importance (or otherwise) of melody, and rhythm;
choice of harmonies (concords, discords, chromaticisms);
exploitation of the piano's *legato* 'singing' qualities – or *staccato* percussive qualities;
use of dynamics;
type of musical texture created;
use of any particular devices or effects;
the standard of technique expected of the performer.

Assignment 51 1 Draw two charts, beginning as those shown below.
On your first chart enter the names of those instruments most likely to be included in one of Haydn's last symphonies or an early orchestral work by Beethoven or Schubert. (Except for the strings, state how many of each type of instrument will be needed.)
On your second chart list the instruments most likely to be required to play a symphony or a symphonic poem by a mid 19th-century composer. (In the woodwind and brass columns, state how many of each type of instrument will most likely be needed.)

The 'Classical orchestra' (c. 1800)			
woodwind	brass	percussion	strings

The mid 19th-century orchestra			
woodwind	brass	percussion	strings

2 Considering the history of the orchestra from c1720 to the present day:
(a) which section has changed the most from the point of view of the development and improvement of its instruments?
(b) in which section (or sections) have the instruments greatly increased in both number and type – offering the composer a much richer variety of tone-colours?
(c) which section has been least affected by change, remained most stable?

Assignment 52

1 In which musical form did Haydn usually structure the third movement of his symphonies?
2 Which form was often used to structure the arias in a Baroque opera?
3 Which form would you expect for the dances in a keyboard suite by Bach?
4 Which form is most often used to build up the first movement of a sonata, symphony, or string quartet by a Classical composer?
5 In which form is the first movement of a Baroque concerto likely to be structured?
6 Name the musical form represented by this plan: A^1 B A^2 C A^3.

Assignment 53

1 Complete these two scales:

(i)  (ii)

2 Complete this series:

Assignment 54

Listen (three or four times) to the sequence of four varied extracts of music recorded on the cassette. As you listen to each extract:

1 (a) Identify as many instruments as you can, and
   (b) describe how their *timbres* are being combined – for instance:
      a blending of timbres of similar kinds;
      a contrasting of timbres of different kinds;
      or perhaps both – in turn.

2 Describe in detail the kind of *texture* which the music presents – for example:

monophonic	few notes at a time
homophonic/chordal	many notes at a time
polyphonic/contrapuntal	smooth, legato
dense, heavy	angular, spiky, staccato
thin, light	. . . and so on.

3 To each extract match one item from each of these categories:

Tonality	Tempo	Type of composition	Period of music
major	Adagio	slow movement of a symphony	Medieval
minor	Andante	a dance	Baroque
modal	Allegro moderato	a fugue	Romantic
atonal	Vivace	a quirky march	20th century

4 Write brief comments on your personal response or reaction to each piece, mentioning qualities or characteristics in the music which interested you – or giving reasons why you think the music failed to interest you.

Assignment 55   **A** Listen to the six varied extracts of music recorded on the cassette, gathering information and discovering answers to the questions on each extract.

Extract 1 (a) With which of the following musical devices does this music begin?
        ostinato;   *imitation*;   *inversion*.

(b) Is the texture of this music monophonic, homophonic, or polyphonic?

(c) By which of these combinations of voices is this music sung?
        male and female voices;   boys' and men's voices;   men's voices.

(d) Which of these terms describes the way the music is performed?
        a cappella;   *bel canto*;   *coloratura*.

(e) Is this extract likely to come from an anthem, a mass, a madrigal, or a part song?

Extract 2 (a) At the beginning of this extract, is the bass played *pizzicato*, *arco*, or *col legno*?

(b) Which of these percussion instruments does the composer feature?
        glockenspiel;   xylophone;   triangle;   celesta.

(c) In which time or metre is this music written?
        simple duple;   simple triple;   compound duple.

(d) When the characteristic dance-rhythm becomes established, which of these rhythmic patterns is repeated?

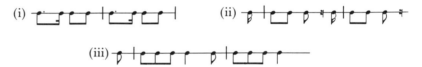

(e) Is this national dance a tango, a waltz, a csárdás, a polka, or a polonaise?

Extract 3 (a) Does the orchestra here consist of strings only, of strings and woodwind, or of strings and brass?

(b) Which of these instruments do you hear playing the continuo part?
        lute;   harp;   harpsichord;   organ.

(c) Is the solo part sung by Maria Callas, Kathleen Ferrier, Alfred Deller, or Placido Domingo?

(d) Which of the following describes this kind of composition?
        recitative;   *aria*;   *chorus*;   *chorale*.

(e) Is this extract taken from an oratorio, an opera, a motet, or a requiem?

Extract 4 (a) What time signature would be printed at the beginning of this music?

(b) Which of the following kinds of drum do you hear?
        kettle drum;   snare drum;   tenor drum;   bass drum.

(c) The key signature contains a single sharp. Is the tonic key of the music: F major, G major, or E minor?

(d) Which of these tempo markings matches this music?
        andante;   *allegretto*;   *presto*.

(e) Is this extract from a concerto, a symphony, a sonata, or a quintet?

(f) What name would be given to this particular movement of the complete work?

Extract 5 (a) Which of the following types of voice do you hear?
mezzo-soprano;   contralto;   countertenor;   tenor.

(b) Which of these terms matches this music?
major;   minor;   modal;   atonal.

(c) Select the time signature which best suits this music:

$$\mathbf{C} \qquad \mathbf{\cent} \qquad \frac{3}{4} \qquad \frac{6}{8}$$

(d) Which of these groups of instruments accompanies the voice?

viol, lute, sackbut	fiddle, viol, harp, shawm

fiddle, viol, lute, harp

Extract 6 (a) Do the various parts in the musical texture move entirely by step, mainly by step but with occasional small leaps, or mostly by very wide leaps?

(b) Is this music performed by a string quartet, by a string sextet, or by a small string orchestra?

(c) Which of these terms matches this music?
modal;   chromatic;   atonal.

(d) In this piece, do the dynamics and also the tempo:
remain the same throughout;
gradually increase throughout; or
continually fluctuate, over a very wide range?

(e) Which of the following best describes the musical style?
Impressionism;   Expressionism;   Neoclassicism.

(f) Various 'colouristic' effects are used. Explain:
pizzicato;   *col legno*;   *sul ponticello*;   *con sordino*.

(g) Describe the mood, or moods, the composer presents in this music.

B Listen to the six extracts again. As you listen to each extract:
(1) note down, from box 1 below, the period when the music was written;
(2) choose the most likely composer, from box 2;
(3) add his country of birth from box 3 (a country may be represented more than once).

1	Medieval (to 1450)	Renaissance (1450–1600)	Baroque (1600–1750)	Classical (1750–1810)	Romantic (1810–1910)	'Modern' (20th Century)

2	Francesco Landini Palestrina Giovanni Gabrieli Handel
	Haydn Beethoven Chopin Wagner
	Smetana Tchaikovsky Debussy Webern Britten

3	Italy Austria Germany France
	Poland Russia (USSR) Bohemia (Czechoslovakia)

Assignment 56	**Using physical space: Canzona**

The *canzona* (also called *canzon*) was a very common type of instrumental piece during the 16th century, often influenced by songs and also by dance music. Spatial arrangement of performing forces was a frequent characteristic of the canzonas of 16th-century Venice: pieces would use two or more different instrumental groups, spaced apart for effect. It is interesting that in the 20th century, composers have also chosen to exploit physical space, often influenced by the ideas of electronic music. You will be familiar with stereophonic and other multi-channel effects. In this assignment, we are exploring this kind of use of physical space in music. |
| **Some ideas to help you** | Compose your music for several groups of instruments which can be spaced around the room in performance. You may like to include only one type of instrument in each group; for example:

    Group 1: woodwind
    Group 2: tuned percussion
    Group 3: non-tuned percussion
    Group 4: strings
    Group 5: brass

(Of course, these are only suggestions; you can use any instruments or voices available.) |
| **Some musical suggestions** | Obviously, musical contrast is going to be a very important device in a spatial piece. Your contrasts need to be:

(1) as **exaggerated** as possible;
(2) they need to use **all** aspects of the music.

For instance, each group could have its own tempo, and perhaps its own style of music.

    Canzonas frequently began with the same rhythmic pattern:

This could be used as the basis for a danced piece to go with your music. The dance could exploit the physical space of the room as the music does. Each group might contain musicians and dancers, who perform together when the music tells them. Or you may decide to have one structure for the music, and a different one for the dance. |
| **Pieces to listen to** | Giovanni Gabrieli: *In ecclesiis* (solo voices, double chorus, instruments);
    Canzona XIII (for three instrumental groups)
Massaino: *Canzon* for 8 trombones
Birtwistle: *Verses for ensembles*
Stockhausen: *Gruppen* ('Groups') for three orchestras
Varèse: *Poème Électronique* |
| **Assignment 57** | **Forwards/backwards/upside-down**

The organization of pitch may also be thought of in terms of space; a *pitch* space. Serialism is the term for a method of organizing pitch first thought up by the composer Arnold Schoenberg. In learning composition, it is useful to know the basic principles of serialism. It is also surprisingly easy to use it to make music. |

The composer uses a series (or set, or note-row) of 12 different pitches, placed in a particular order, as the main material. For instance:

These pitches may be used in any octave, but must remain in the same order. Notes may be used one at a time, or two or more at once. The composer also may use three other related versions of the series. These are the inversion (or upside-down) version:

the retrograde (or backwards) version:

and the retrograde-inversion (upside-down *and* backwards at the same time):

(You can hear all the above versions of the series on the cassette.)

Listen to the *Prelude* and *Gavotte and Musette* from Schoenberg's Suite for piano, Opus 25; and the first five minutes or so of Berg's Violin Concerto. Compare their quite different uses of serialism.

Serialism can be extremely useful, especially as it removes the necessity to be continually concerned with the choice of notes, and enables the composer to concentrate on 'higher-level' decisions. The following points need to be remembered:

(1) Serialism of pitch doesn't prevent individualism; it is an extremely flexible approach, with plenty of decisions to be made apart from shaping the series – for instance, those to do with rhythm and structure.

(2) Although Schoenberg used all 12 notes in a series, effective use can be made of series with less than 12 notes.

(3) A great deal of effort should be spent on designing the series to suit your needs, so that it contains the right combination of intervals in the right order.

Stage 1   Shape a series of six notes. Then, using an ensemble of three people, give each instrument two notes from the set. Use any spare instruments as soloists who can improvise with the material over the top of repeated versions of the series played by the others.

Make several different recordings of your note-series, and then compare the different versions. Discuss the characteristics of your material.

Stage 2   Then try a similar approach with a twelve-note series. Improvise everything else about the music. For instance:

(1) dynamics;

(2) octave placing of the notes;

(3) use of *tremolando, staccato*, and other ways of articulating a note;

(4) actual note lengths.

(You can hear a version of this assignment on the cassette.)

Assignment 58   **Rock riffs**

Riff is a term commonly used in pop and rock music to describe a repeating musical pattern, often in the bass. This assignment is a performing and composing one, with a number of stages.

Stage 1   Perform each of the following riffs, on any instrument:

Stage 2   Experiment with playing several of the riffs at once. They will all fit together, and can be played in any octave. You can also experiment with varying the riff in simple ways. For instance, the first one might be varied as follows:

Stage 3   The riffs are constructed out of the following scale, with D as its tonic:

Use the notes of the scale to compose a main tune, either for solo instrument, or for voice; you can write your own words for the voice if you wish. Any music you compose will fit on top of the above riffs, because it uses the same scale.

Stage 4   Add some accompanying rhythmic patterns on a drum kit, drum machine, or any percussion instruments available. Here are some suggestions for suitable patterns:

Stage 5   Put together a final shape for your piece. Decide:
  (i) whether or not to have an introduction and an ending;
  (ii) in which order the riffs will enter (perhaps one by one – or several starting at the same time).

Record a final performance of the whole thing, and listen to it.
(A version of this assignment is on the cassette.)

Assignment 59

Pentatonic

Study and play the following Chinese tune; on the cassette it is played by the *di* (a Chinese flute), but it will work on any melodic instrument.

This tune is mainly based on a simple 5-note (pentatonic) scale which can be written out like this:

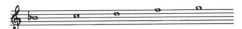

Spend some time improvising, using only the notes of this scale (in any octave) and listening carefully all the time.

Now compose a tune of your own, using the same scale. Give your tune six different phrases. If you like, decide in advance how many notes in each phrase (say, five). As a first stage, make all the notes equal in length. Write out your six-phrase tune and play it – either on your own, or, better still, with your fellow musicians.

There are two more things to do to your tune:

(a) Decide on the note-lengths; experiment with different versions.

(b) Try putting some interesting decoration between the notes. Here are three suggestions about this:

(1) Add some two-note figures, like this:

(2) Slide between notes (or include all the notes in between if your instrument cannot slide), like this:

(3) Trill on some of the notes, like this:

Finally, record the ensemble playing your finished tune. It would be fascinating if different players decorated the tune at different times. Also, you can experiment with changing the order of the phrases – with pentatonic tunes there is much greater flexibility about the order of notes than with major/minor ones.

 (There is a version of this assignment on the cassette.)

Assignment 60   **African drumming patterns**

One of the most interesting characteristics of African drumming is that although it often sounds complex, the individual drums are playing relatively simple rhythm patterns. It is the mixing together of them that makes the music sound interesting. In this assignment, we will gradually build up an interesting texture for drums (or other percussion instruments) and help our aural development by listening to it.

Each player (or group of players) has a rhythmic pattern as follows:

When each player can satisfactorily play his/her own pattern, the texture can be built up. This is best done in two stages:

Stage 1   The players enter one by one. Once they have entered, they continue repeating their pattern until all are playing.

Stage 2   At a given signal, players move to the next pattern to the one with which they began (after the 5th pattern, move back to the first).

At successive signals, players can continue changing patterns until the initial one is reached again.

All the time, players should listen very carefully to themselves and to all the others. Make a recording, and afterwards listen to it.

Assignment 61   Listen to extracts from some of these different types and styles of music:

traditional jazz	ragtime	blues	modern jazz
rock reggae	rhythm 'n' blues	folk music	a musical
African music	Eastern music (e.g. from India, China or Japan)		

As you listen, write brief comments on the music. For example, these could include:

- the types of **instruments** and/or **voices** used (are any being featured in particular? against what kind of accompaniment or backing?)
- the kind of **beat** and **rhythm** used (how many beats to a bar? is syncopation used? is the beat strongly emphasized – or, perhaps, almost imperceptible?)
- **texture** – describe the kind of texture the music presents (see the suggestions for Assignment 54 part 2, on page 31)
- **structure** – is the music being built up according to any particular musical form or structure? Are any special **musical devices** used – such as repetition, variation, sequence, ostinato?
- **style** – name the style of the music, and/or its country of origin
- **mood** – is a definite mood being presented? (If so, describe it, and mention the musical means being used to achieve it)

Assignment 62

piano sonata	trio sonata	plainchant	jazz	estampie

string quartet   'broken' consort   symphonic poem

Elizabethan madrigals   concert overture   French overture

divertimento   atonality   organum   opera

sonata form   harpsichord suite   figured bass   ground bass

concerto grosso   electronic music   chorale prelude

serialism   nationalism   oratorio

fantasia for viols   Alberti bass   'character' piece for piano

During which period did each of these forms, types and styles of music first become popular with composers? On a sheet of paper (turned sideways to give sufficient width) draw a chart similar to the one below, and add each item from the box to the correct column of your chart.

Medieval (to 1450)	Renaissance (1450–1600)	Baroque (1600–1750)	Classical (1750–1810)	Romantic (1810–1910)	'Modern' (20th Century)

Assignment 63

1 For which instruments did Bach write keyboard compositions?
2 Briefly describe the way in which each of these produces its sounds.
3 Describe one of Bach's keyboard compositions in some detail.

Assignment 64

Explain each of these terms, in some way connected with an oratorio, cantata, or Passion:

recitative	aria	arioso	chorus	chorale

Assignment 65

Explain these terms, in some way connected with a Baroque concerto:

concertino	ripieno	continuo	ritornello	tutti

Assignment 66

Explain each of these terms, in some way connected with sonata form:

exposition	development	recapitulation	coda
first subject	bridge passage	second subject	codetta

Assignment 67   Name (together with their composers):
(a) two symphonies which involve voices
(b) two concertos featuring more than one soloist
(c) three sets of variations
(d) three madrigals of different kinds
(e) two church anthems of different kinds
(f) three suites – one for keyboard, one for string orchestra, and one for full orchestra or brass band or military band
(g) two quintets for strings + one other instrument
(h) three compositions inspired by Shakespeare's *Romeo and Juliet*
(i) two 'serious' compositions influenced in some way by jazz
(j) three pieces in impressionist style
(k) a composition in pointillist style
(l) a 'rock opera'

Assignment 68   Name (together with the composer concerned):
(a) a set of preludes and fugues
(b) a nationalist opera
(c) a 20th-century opera in English
(d) a song-cycle for voice and piano, and another for voice and orchestra
(e) a requiem
(f) a serial (12-note) composition
(g) an aleatoric (or 'chance-choice') composition
(h) a piece of electronic music, or a work which combines electronic sounds with voices and/or instruments, live or on tape

Assignment 69   Name three composers of:

(a) madrigals	(f) Lieder
(b) pieces for virginals	(g) 19th-century 'character' pieces for piano
(c) motets	(h) symphonic poems (or tone poems)
(d) concerti grossi	(i) serial (12-note) compositions
(e) oratorios	(j) modern jazz

Assignment 70   Each of these (approximate) dates marks a 'crisis point' in the history of music:

c1300   c1600   c1900

Choose one of these dates, and describe some of the important changes which took place in musical style.

Assignment 71   Which type or period of music interests you the most? Describe in detail a composition which you have thoroughly enjoyed listening to. Give reasons why this music has impressed you.

Assignment 72   When you are given an extract of music to listen to, and asked to identify the musical period when it was composed:
(1) Which period or style do you find easiest to recognize and identify?
(2) Mention some of the typical sounds, or 'fingerprints' of style, which make it easy for you to identify music of this particular period.

Part Two: Practice Scores and Assignments

Some general hints on following a score

Before listening

- Always prepare your listening first by carefully investigating the score.
- Discover which instruments (and/or voices) are taking part. They will be named, usually in a foreign language, on the first page of the score; on other pages, abbreviated names may be used.
- Look at the tempo (speed) marking – this will give you some idea of how quickly your eye must travel to keep up with the music.
- Note the time signature, indicating the number of beats to a bar.
- Look through carefully for repeat signs, or any other indications that sections of music are to be repeated.
- Notice where any Italian words or abbreviations are used in the score; Make sure you know the meaning of these, and any other musical signs and symbols, before following the score.

As you follow the score

- Always use your eyes and ears to help each other – matching what you *see* to what you *hear.*
- Always be ready for page-turns. It is better to turn over slightly in advance, rather than leave it too late and be left behind.
- Notice at a glance the number of systems (one, or more) to a page. Two or more systems may be separated by slanting lines (⫽) or merely by a break in the vertical line down the left side of the score.
- Within each system, those instruments playing will be arranged in 'score order' – woodwind, brass, percussion, strings – with thick brackets down the left side of the score, and/or a break in the bar-lines, grouping the staves according to these orchestral sections.
- As you listen, identify the sounds of instruments playing the most interesting part at the time, and swiftly locate their position within the system according to score order. (In many scores, for much of the time, you will find that the main interest lies in the first violin part.)
- Certain 'landmarks' in the score will help you to check that you are keeping your place (or to find it again should you get lost!); for example: wide leaps; trills, and other ornaments; a distinctive rhythmic pattern or a group of notes which is repeated; sequences; certain dynamic markings; a percussion entry (perhaps a drum-roll, or a cymbal crash); a loud *tutti* after a sparsely scored passage, or vice versa.
- Be prepared for repeats. Note the point to which your eye needs to *return* (perhaps keeping a finger in the page to negotiate a swift turn-back).

If you should lose your place . . .

- Quickly make sure you haven't miscounted the number of systems to a page, or missed a repeat and should have gone back. If not, it is most likely that you have fallen behind – so skip forward and find a 'landmark' in the score that you are sure you will recognize. *Listen all the time*, and as soon as your ears tell you the music is arriving at that point – quickly latch on, and continue to follow the score.

Score 1 Anthem: *If Ye Love Me*   *Thomas Tallis (c.1505–1585)*

The Tudor composer Thomas Tallis lived through the reigns of Henry VIII, Edward VI, Mary Tudor, and more than half the reign of Elizabeth I. At times when the Roman Catholic religion held sway, he composed motets and masses to words in Latin; in Protestant times, he composed anthems and services to English words.

Assignment 1 **A** Before listening to this anthem, look carefully through the score. Notice the types of voices involved, and that the tenor part is written in the treble clef – one octave higher than the actual sounds.

B Listen to the music, following the score.

Assignment 2

1 In the opening bars of this anthem, is the musical texture homophonic (chordal) or polyphonic (contrapuntal)?

2 With what kind of cadence does Tallis end the anthem? Is it:

plagal	imperfect	perfect	interrupted	tierce de Picardie

3 Much of the beauty and serenity of this music is due to its simplicity. But if, when following the score, you followed only the highest part, you may have been puzzled – or even have become 'lost'. The highest voice-part does not always sing the highest pitches. Investigate the score, and find instances where there is an 'overlapping' or 'crossing' of the parts:
   (a) between treble and alto;   (b) between alto and tenor.

Assignment 3

1 At bar 5, Tallis introduces a 'point of imitation'. In which order do the four voice-groups enter with this melodic idea? Describe the texture.

2 Give the bar numbers where Tallis brings in other points of imitation later on. In each instance, mention the order in which the voice-groups enter.

3 (a) What is an *anthem*?
   (b) Is this a 'full anthem', or a 'verse anthem'?

4 Listen to this anthem again, following the score. Be especially aware of: (i) points of imitation, and the order in which the voice-groups take up each point; and also (ii) occasions when there is an overlapping of parts – particularly between treble and alto.

Score 2 'Hallelujah Chorus' from *Messiah*   *Handel (1685–1759)*

Before listening:

Assignment 4 1 Here, you will be following a vocal score of a well-known piece for chorus and orchestra. What is a 'vocal score'?
2 How many groups of voices will be taking part? What types of voices?
3 Name the clef used for each of these voice-parts.
4 Which part is printed an octave higher than the voices will actually sound?
5 (a) In which key is this chorus written?
(b) How many beats to a bar are there in this music?
(c) What is the meaning of *Allegro*?

Assignment 5 1 Look through the pages of this score, discovering how many systems there are on each page. What is a 'system'?
2 In this score, how can you tell at a glance how many systems each page carries?

Chorus – Hallelujah!

Assignment 6

1   (a) Name the highest note sung by the sopranos during this chorus. In which bar does it occur?
    (b) Name the lowest note sung by the basses. In which bar does it occur?
2   When the voices enter for the first time, is the musical texture homophonic (chordal) or polyphonic (contrapuntal)?
3   (a) In which bar do all the voices first sing in unison?
    (b) Are the accompanying instruments also in unison, or do they provide a chordal background?
4   Describe the kind of musical texture Handel presents:
        (a) from bar 22 to bar 32;
        (b) from the end of bar 33 to the beginning of bar 41.
5   At bar 42 begins a *fugato* (a passage which sets off in the style of a fugue, but is less strict and less complete than a true fugue). The subject (or theme) of this fugato is presented four times. In which order do the voice-groups enter with the subject?
6   (a) At which point during the 'Hallelujah Chorus' does the climax occur?
    (b) Describe how the music builds up to this climax.
7   With which of the following kinds of cadence does Handel end the chorus?

| perfect | imperfect | plagal | interrupted | tierce de Picardie |

8   Which instruments, other than string instruments, accompany the voices during this chorus?

Assignment 7

Throughout this vocal score of the 'Hallelujah Chorus' the voice-parts are printed in 'open score' – that is, with a separate stave for each part. Here are the voice-parts of bars 4–7 printed in 'short score' – with the four voice-parts printed on two staves only:

(a) Six of the chords are already identified beneath the music (D = chord of D major, and so on). Identify the remaining chords.
(b) Write out the voice-parts of the next four bars (8–11) in 'short score'. You will need to transpose the tenor notes down an octave to the bass clef. Write all notes for sopranos and tenors with their stems upwards, and all notes for altos and basses with their stems downwards.
(Hint: write the bass part *before* you write the tenor part.)

Assignment 8

Listen to the 'Hallelujah Chorus' again. Choose a voice-part other than the soprano, and follow that part throughout.

Assignment 9

1   *Messiah* is Handel's most popular oratorio. What is an oratorio?
2   Besides choruses, what other types of piece would you expect to hear during an oratorio?
3   For each of these oratorios, name the composer and his nationality:
        (a) *Elijah*   (b) *Belshazzar's Feast*   (c) *The Dream of Gerontius*
        (d) *Judas Maccabæus*   (e) *The Creation*   (f) *The Childhood of Christ*

Score 3 Third Movement from String Quartet in D major, Opus 64, No. 5

Haydn (1732–1809)

This is the Minuet and Trio from Haydn's 'Lark' Quartet (so called because of the soaring theme played by the first violin at the opening of the first movement). As you follow this score, be ready for all repeats!

Menuetto D.C.

Assignment 10

1. In which bar do all four instruments first play in unison?
2. Name the interval between second violin and viola from the end of bar 20 to the end of bar 23.
3. Which instrument has the tune at the beginning of the Trio?
4. Who takes over the tune? In which bar?
5. At which bar of the Trio is the tune played by (a) cello, (b) viola?
6. Is the Trio chordal, or contrapuntal, in style?
7. Is the Trio designed in binary form, or in ternary form?
8. Write out the first twelve notes played by the viola in the second part of the Trio – but in the treble clef instead of the viola clef.
9. Mention two ways in which the Trio contrasts with the Minuet.
10. Explain each of the following:
    Allegretto   *Menuetto D.C.*   *Fine*   𝆋   𝄽   ♪   ∾ (bar 25)
11. Listen to this Minuet and Trio again, following the score.

Assignment 11   **A** *Before listening*   Look carefully through the score, noticing repeat signs.
   B *As you follow the score*   The music is quite brisk, so when the upper
   part is particularly 'busy' you may find it best to follow the lower part.

Assignment 12

1. Which instrument plays this music? How does this instrument's way of producing sounds differ from that of the clavichord?

2. At the end of the piece, the player (George Malcolm) cheekily adds notes of his own to Daquin's music. Write these 'extra' notes on a five-line stave.

3. In which bars does Malcolm vary the sound by using a 'harp' stop?

4. Name another famous player of the same instrument.

5. Mention another composer who lived in the same country as Daquin and wrote many pieces for the same instrument.

6. (a) Name three kinds of ornament printed in this score.
   (b) What kind of ornament is fully written out in bar 69?

7. Is this music in ternary form, rondo form, or variation form?

8. In spring, the two notes of the cuckoo's call sound a major 3rd. But the interval gradually narrows until, by summer, the notes form a minor 3rd. At which time of year are we hearing Daquin's cuckoo (bars 1–3)?

9. What name is given to music like this, which is descriptive?

10. Give the title and composer of another piece which features a cuckoo.

Assignment 13

1 In which key does this extract begin?

2 On a five-line stave, draw, and name, four different kinds of clef used in this score. After each clef, add the note middle C.

3 Name each of the instruments which take part in this Piano Quartet by Brahms.

4 Which of these instruments first plays the melody? Which clef is used? Write the first four notes (a) in the treble clef, (b) in the bass clef. (In each case, include key signature and time signature.)

5 Name the second instrument to play the melody. At which bar does it begin?

6 Is the melody now: (i) inverted,
                       (ii) decorated, or
                       (iii) presented exactly as at first?

7 In which bar does the fourth instrument enter? Which instrument is it?

8 In this extract from Brahms's score, does the piano eventually take over the melody, or does it accompany throughout?

9 From the end of bar 26 to the end of bar 27, are the two highest-sounding instruments playing in 3rds, in 2nds, in 6ths, or in unison?

10 Explain each of the following:
Andante ℭ   *poco* *f* *espress.* *dim.* ⸺ ⟨ ⟩ ⁀₃

11 In bars 27–33, why does the piano part use two bass clefs – rather than (as is more usual) a bass clef and a treble clef?

Score 6 **Second Movement from Divertimento** *Mozart (1756–1791)*
No. 1 in E♭ major, K113

Divertimento is an Italian word meaning 'entertainment', 'amusement', or 'diversion'. In Mozart's day, a divertimento was an instrumental work in several movements (from three to eight or more) which combined features of the symphony and the suite. The music, light and entertaining in style, was usually intended for performance by an ensemble of solo instruments. Another, similar, type of composition was the *serenade* ('evening music').

Mozart's Divertimento in E flat, K113, has four movements (the third movement is printed on page 24).

Before listening:

Assignment 14
1 Look carefully through the score of this second movement. How many systems are there on each page? How many staves are there to each system?
2 How could you tell at a glance how many systems each page carries – even if there were no parallel slanting lines (⫽) printed in between?
3 List, in English, each type of instrument taking part.
4 To which section of the orchestra does each instrument belong?
5 At which bar of the score will all the instruments be heard playing together for the first time?
6 Which bars of the score will be played by string instruments ònly?

Assignment 15
(a) Which instruments taking part are 'transposing' instruments?
(b) Write out the first bar played by each of these instruments,
(i) as the notes are written, (ii) as they will actually sound.

60

After listening:

Assignment 16

1 (a) What is the tonic key of this movement?

(b) To which key has the music modulated by bar 18? How is this key related to the tonic key of the movement?

2 (a) In which bar of the score do instruments play entirely in unison?

(b) Give the letter-names of the notes played in this bar.

3 (a) Give the bar numbers where the second horn plays an arpeggio.

(b) In which bar is the first clarinettist heard playing a complete rising scale of B flat major?

4 Which of the following matches the recording you have heard?

(i) played by 4 solo woodwinds and 4 solo strings;

(ii) played by 4 solo wind instruments and string orchestra;

(iii) played by 4 solo wind instruments and 5 solo strings.

Menuetto da capo.

Assignment 17

1. In which key is the Minuet? In which key is the Trio?
2. (a) Explain: *Clarinetti in B, Corni in Es.*
   (b) Name the first note *sounded* by each of these instruments.
3. Name the interval sounded between (a) the two clarinets in bars 9–12
   (b) the horns in bars 1–4 (c) the second violin and the viola in bar 24.
4. Mention three ways in which the Trio contrasts with the Minuet.
5. In which musical form is this whole movement built up?
6. In which musical form is the Minuet section?
7. In which musical form is the Trio section?

Score 8 Slow Movement from Violin Concerto in D major, Opus 35

Tchaikovsky (1840–1893)

Tchaikovsky composed his Violin Concerto in 1878. This expressive slow movement entitled *Canzonetta* (Italian for 'short song') was sketched in a single day. As you follow this score, use eyes and ears together to identify instruments playing the most interesting phrases, immediately locating their position within the system according to score order. This is virtually the complete slow movement – after the final bar of this score a sixteen-bar link leads into the third and final movement of the Concerto.

Assignment 18

1 (a) Complete this chart, detailing the instruments included in this movement:

Italian name	Abbreviation	English name	Section
2 Flauti	Fl.	2 flutes	woodwind

(b) Which instruments on your chart do not play during page 66?

(c) And which do not play during page 68?

2 In which bar of the score is each of the following first heard?

(a) the solo violin; (b) the second horn; (c) cellos;

(d) double basses; (e) first bassoon; (f) first flute.

3 Explain each of these details from Tchaikovsky's score:

Andante	*pp*	*più **f***	con sord.	*molto espress.*	
cresc.	*dim.*	1.	rit.	pizz.	arco

Assignment 19

1 The first twelve bars of this movement form an introduction. Which instrument plays the tune during these bars?

2 (a) The main theme of the movement begins one beat before bar 13. In which key is this melody?

(b) What contrast is there in sound, after the music of the introduction?

3 A link passage begins at bar 34. Which of these words matches the music?

sequence; *imitation*; *ostinato*; *inversion*.

4 The link leads to a contrasting theme. At which bar does it begin? In which key is it?

5 (a) At which bar does the music of the introduction reappear?

(b) Which instruments are involved?

6 (a) In which bar does the main theme return?

(b) How is it different from when it was first heard?

7 The music of the introduction is heard for a third time. At which bar?

Assignment 20

(a) Explain Tchaikovsky's metronome marking.

(b) Does the performance of this movement on the cassette obey this – or is the speed much faster or much slower?

Score 9   Finale from Symphony No. 31 in D major ('Hornsignal')

Haydn (1732–1809)

Haydn's Symphony No. 31, composed in 1765, is known as the 'Hornsignal' because of a fanfare and an ancient hunting call ('signal') sounded by the horns during the first movement. The fanfare is heard again at the end of the Finale. In this symphony, Haydn uses four horns (rather than two, as was usual at the time) and their parts are fiendishly difficult to play – in fact the horn players of the Esterházy court orchestra, for whom this music was written, must have been among the finest in all Europe.

The recording of this movement on the cassette is of Antal Dorati conducting the Philharmonia Hungarica – an orchestra, formed in 1957, of Hungarian refugees. Between 1970 and 1973 these musicians made a complete recording of all Haydn's symphonies.

As you follow this score, watch out for all repeats – and be ready for the page-turn during the *Presto* coda! In addition to the instruments named in the score, you will also hear a harpsichord filling out the harmonies, and a bassoon discreetly doubling the cello part.

71

Assignment 21

1 In which musical form does Haydn design the theme and each variation?

2 Besides harpsichord, which instruments are heard playing in this Finale? List the instruments in 'score order'; then draw brackets down the left side of your list, marking off the instruments according to sections of the orchestra.

3 In which bar of this score do all the instruments first play together?

4 Which orchestral section is not represented in this Finale?

5 Listen to the music again, and list the instruments which Haydn features as soloists, in the order they are heard during the variations.

6   **melody** • **harmony** • **rhythm** • **timbre**

Do you think all the above musical ingredients are equally important in this piece – or do some come over more strongly than others?

Wagner composed this music in 1870 as a birthday present for his wife, Cosima, and the piece was first performed by a group of fifteen players (with Wagner conducting) outside her bedroom door at their villa at Triebschen on Christmas morning, 1870. The title refers to their son Siegfried (then one-and-a-half years old) and the music is based on various leading-motives from Wagner's opera *Siegfried*, together with a cradle-song.

In the recording on the cassette of this extract from the score, the music is performed by a group of solo players - one player per part.

Assignment 22		(a) List, in English, the instruments mentioned on page 79.
		(b) Which of these instruments is not heard during this extract?

Assignment 23	1	(a) Name the tonic key of this music.
		(b) Explain: *Con moto ma tranquillo*; *più rallent.*; *a tempo*.
	2	Why, on some pages of this score, are there extra (curved) brackets down the left-hand side?
	3	(a) In which bar does the cellist first use double-stopping?
		(b) Name the notes sounded, and also the interval which they form.
		(c) Name the notes sounded by the viola in the same bar.

Assignment 24		This assignment might be entitled 'Score search':
	1	Give the bar number where each of these instruments is first heard:
		(a) double bass; (b) oboe; (c) second clarinet; (d) bassoon;
		(e) flute; (f) first horn.
	2	Give the bar number(s) where:
		(a) the double bass is played *pizzicato* for the first time:
		(b) the viola is played *pizzicato* in double-stopping;
		(c) the cello's notes are written in the tenor clef;
		(d) the bassoon's notes are written in the tenor clef;
		(e) the viola plays a trill on the note C♯;
		(f) the second horn part is written in the bass clef;
		(g) one of the horn players changes from horn in E to horn in B;
		(h) the oboe doubles the first violin an octave lower;
		(i) first clarinet and first violin play two bars in unison;
		(j) the double bass plays a tonic pedal, several bars long.

Assignment 25	1	The figure played by the first violin at bar 4 is heard again at bar 43. Which instruments play it then?
	2	(a) Which instrument first plays this phrase?
		(b) The phrase is then freely imitated by several other instruments. Name the instruments in the order in which they take up the phrase. (Eyes *and* ears will help you to answer this question.)
	3	The figure played by the second violin at bar 63 begins another series of imitations. Name, in order, the instruments which imitate this figure.

Assignment 26		Name the interval formed by the two notes played by:

(a) the flute in bar 49;   (d) the viola in bar 41;

(b) the double bass in bar 25;   (e) the oboe in bar 44;

(c) the second violin in bar 20; (f) the viola in bar 64.

Assignment 27		Write out bars 45 and 46 of the second clarinet part – (a) as they are written; (b) using the correct key signature, at the pitch they sound.

Assignment 28	1	If you can, listen to this extract played in a version which uses a full string section (rather than, as here, one player per part). Which version do you prefer? Why?
	2	Listen to an extract from another orchestral piece by Wagner, following the score (e.g. *Siegfried's Funeral March*, page 72 of 'Score-reading'). Mention some of the contrasts between that piece and the *Siegfried Idyll*.

Score 11 — First Movement (bars 1–124) from Symphony No. 5 in C minor, Opus 67

Beethoven (1770–1827)

Beethoven composed his Fifth Symphony in 1807–8. The first movement is in sonata form (see the diagram on page 93) and this extract of the score shows the exposition section. The entire first movement is dominated by a four-note rhythmic motive (*x*, on the left). This is hammered out twice by strings and clarinets in unison. Then Beethoven builds up a musical paragraph, distributing the motive among the upper strings – beginning with second violins (bar 6), violas (bar 7), first violins (bar 8). Notice, in bar 7, that although you lower your eye to the violas' stave, the pitch of their notes is in fact higher than that of the second violins.

As you follow this score, be ready for all page-turns – especially the first (bars 11/12).

I.

Assignment 29 Explain the following details from Beethoven's score:

Allegro con brio				$(\downarrow = 108)$ $\frac{2}{4}$
	Clarinetti in $\begin{bmatrix} B \\ Si\flat \end{bmatrix}$		Corni in $\begin{bmatrix} Es \\ Mi\flat \end{bmatrix}$	
1. (e.g. bar 32)	⌢			sf dolce

Assignment 30 For each instrument below give (1) the number of the bar in which it is first heard, and (2) the pitch of the first note the instrument sounds.

    (a) second clarinet   (d) kettle drum
    (b) first trumpet   (e) second flute
    (c) first bassoon   (f) second horn

Assignment 31 1 In the first system of the score on page 88, cellos and double basses are given separate staves. Why is this? When does this occur again?
    2 When, after bar 83, do the first violins and second violins cease to play in octaves or in unison?
    3 In this score, do the trumpets behave as transposing instruments? Why?
    4 Explain the meaning of *a 2* printed above the horn stave at bar 18. Why is *a 2* not also printed above the trumpet stave?

Assignment 32 Beethoven builds up the first movement of his Fifth Symphony in sonata form:

Exposition (presentation)			Development (discussion) moving through new keys,	Recapitulation (restatement)			Coda
First subject (tonic)	Bridge (changing key)	Second subject (in a new key)	discussing, developing, combining and opposing ideas from the exposition	First subject (tonic)	Bridge (now altered)	Second subject (*tonic*)	to round off

This extract from the score gives the exposition section of the movement.
    (1) In which bar, do you think, does the second subject begin?
    (2) In which key is it? How is this related to the tonic key?
    (3) The first part of the second subject is built up in four-bar phrases. Name the instruments which, in turn, play the first five phrases.
    (4) The rhythm of motive *x*, from the first subject, is still present during the second subject. Which instruments play it during the first five phrases of the second subject?
    (5) In which bars of this exposition section is motive *x* heard for the last time? Which instruments play it?

Assignment 33 (a) Write the bassoon notes of bar 104, first in the bass clef, and then in the treble clef.
    (b) Write the clarinet parts of bar 103 at the pitch they actually sound.
    (c) Write the horn parts of bars 18–21 at the pitch they actually sound.

Assignment 34 Listen again to the movement by Haydn (page 71) and then this music by Beethoven. Which do you find the most interesting to listen to? Which score do you find the most interesting to follow? Give reasons for your choices.

Score 12
No. 3 of *Five Pieces for Orchestra* — *Anton Webern (1883–1945)*
Opus 10 (composed 1911–13)

This 20th-century score is very different in both style and appearance from the other scores in this book. Notice which instruments take part (see also the boxes opposite) and the 'score order'. As usual, woodwind and brass come at the top of each system, and strings at the bottom with percussion above them. But between, come several other instruments. Webern treats all these instruments as soloists. The mood is set by several instruments providing a background of bell-like sounds supported by occasional, distant drum-rolls. Against this background, other instruments – separately, or in combination – trace brief melodic shapes. The result is a fabric of sound which consists of scintillating dabs of instrumental colour – described by Stravinsky as Webern's 'dazzling diamonds'.

III.

Webern's orchestra for his *Five Pieces for Orchestra*, Opus 10

Flöte (flute)	Schlagwerk (percussion):
Kleine Flöte (piccolo)	Glockenspiel
Oboe	Xylophon
Klarinette in B (clarinet in B♭)	Herdenglocken (cowbells)
Klarinette in Es (clarinet in E♭)	Tiefe Glocken (tubular bells)
Horn in F	Triangel
Trompete in B (trumpet in B♭)	Becken (cymbals)
Posaune (trombone)	Kleine Trommel (snare drum)
Harmonium	Grosse Trommel (bass drum)
Celesta	Solo-Geige (solo violin)
Mandoline	Solo-Bratsche (solo viola)
Gitarre (guitar)	Solo-Violoncell (solo cello)
Harfe (harp)	Solo-Kontrabass (solo double bass)

Terms used in the score

sehr langsam, very slow
äusserst ruhig, extremely calm
mit Dämpfer, with mute
ohne Dämpfer, without mute
einige tiefe, a few low (bells)
kaum hörbar, barely audible
continuierlich mit vielen Glocken, continually with many bells
verklingend, fading away
zögernd, hesitating
drängend, pressing forward
leise, gentle